C000258778

Text: *Carl Rogers*
Photographs: *Carl Rogers, Shutterstock, Dreamstime*

Design: *Carl Rogers*

© Northern Eye Books Limited 2017

Carl Rogers has asserted his rights under the Copyright, Designs and Patents Act, 1988 to be identified as the authors of this work. All rights reserved.

This book contains mapping data licensed from the Ordnance Survey with the permission of the Controller of Her Majesty's Stationery Office. © Crown copyright 2017 All rights reserved. Licence number 100047867

Ordnance Survey Licensed Mapping

Partner

Northern Eye Books

Northern Eye Books
ISBN 978-1-908632-38-8

A CIP catalogue record for this book is available from the British Library.

www.northerneyebooks.co.uk
www.top10walks.co.uk

Cover: *Looking down Mosedale to Yewbarrow from Pillar (route 8)*

Warning!
Walking and scrambling on the fells can be dangerous and carries the risk of personal injury or death. Do not attempt these walks unless you have suitable experience or training. Conditions can change rapidly, particularly on the high fells, and it is important that walkers have the ability to assess both the conditions and the associated risks.

The routes described in this book are undertaken at the reader's own risk. Walkers should take into account their level of fitness, wear suitable footwear and clothing, and carry food and water. It is also advisable to take the relevant OS map with you in case you get lost and leave the area covered by our maps.

Whilst every care has been taken to ensure the accuracy of the route directions, the publishers cannot accept responsibility for errors or omissions, or for changes in the details given. Nor can the publisher and copyright owners accept responsibility for any consequences arising from the use of this book.

If you find any inaccuracies in either the text or maps, please write or email us at the address below. Thank you.

First published in 2016 by
Northern Eye Books Limited
Northern Eye Books, Tattenhall, Cheshire CH3 9PX
Email: tony@northerneyebooks.com
For sales enquiries, please call 01928 723 744

Twitter: @CarlMarabooks
@Northerneyeboo
@Top10walks

Contents

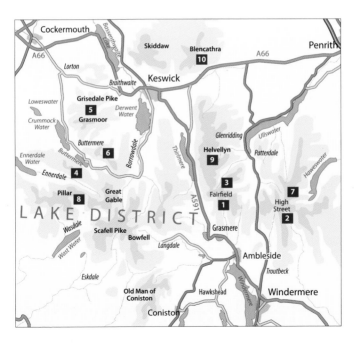

England's largest National Park

The **Lake District National Park** is the largest and most popular of the thirteen National Parks in England and Wales. Created as one of Britain's first National Parks in 1951, its role is to 'conserve and enhance' the natural beauty, wildlife and culture of this iconic English landscape, not just for residents and visitors today but for future generations, too.

Remarkably, the National Park contains every scrap of England's land over 3,000 feet, including its highest mountain, Scafell Pike. Packed within the Park's 885 square miles are numerous peaks and fells, over 400 lakes and tarns, around 50 dales, six National Nature Reserves, and more than 100 Sites of Special Scientific Interest — all publicly accessible on over 1,800 miles of footpaths and other rights of way. It's no surprise then, that the Lake District attracts an estimated 15 million visitors a year.

Lakeland ridges

The Lakeland Fells have some of the finest ridge walks in the country. Exploring these ridges offers fell walking at its most satisfying — staying high, taking in several summits and enjoying the spectacular settings.

Many of the Lake District's ridge walks have become classics, like the grassy edges of the Fairfield and Kentmere Horseshoes, or the rocky aretes of Striding Edge and Swirral Edge, and the aptly named Sharp Edge of Blencathra.

> "[The fells], towering above each other, or lifting themselves in ridges like the waves of a tumultuous sea ... are surpassed by none."
>
> William Wordsworth

Striding Edge

TOP 10 **Walks:** Ridge Walks

The ten routes outlined in the following pages are amongst the very best ridge walks to be enjoyed on the Lakeland Fells. Some are well known classics like the Fairfield or Kentmere Horseshoes, while others are surprisingly well kept secrets like the wonderful Mosedale Horseshoe, the Rough Crag ridge, or the circuit of Deepdale. Also included are Lakeland's most challenging ridge scrambles: Helvellyn's Striding Edge and Swirral Edge, and the dramatic Sharp Edge on Blencathra.

Fairfield Horseshoe — page 8

Kentmere Horseshoe — page 14

Deepdale Horseshoe — page 20

High Stile ridge — page 26

Coledale Horseshoe

Little Dale Round

High Street by Rough Crag

Mosedale Horseshoe

SCRAMBLE

Striding & Swirral Edges

SCRAMBLE

Blencathra's ridges

Fairfield's grassy ridge stretches away into the cloud

Fairfield Horseshoe

Low Sweden Bridge – Low Pike – High Pike – Dove Crag –
Hart Crag – Fairfield – Great Rigg – Heron Pike – Nab Scar

What to expect:
Good paths on a broad, high ridge. Steep descent

Distance: 18.25 kilometres/11½ miles

Ascent/descent: 1,066 metres/3,500 feet

Start: Pay and Display car park at the northern end of Ambleside, on the A591.

Grid ref: NY 376 046

Ordnance Survey Map: OL 5 The English Lakes North-eastern area, and OL 7 The English Lakes South-eastern area

Wainwrights: Low Pike, High Pike, Dove Crag, Hart Crag, Fairfield, Great Rigg, Heron Pike, Nab Scar

Walk outline

Low Sweden Bridge provides the key for gaining the ridge that rises above Scandale. Once reached, this entertaining ridge takes you over progressively higher summits from Low Pike over High Pike, Dove Crag, Hart Crag and eventually the lofty plateau of Fairfield. From here the western arm of the horseshoe is followed in a southerly direction over Great Rigg, Heron Pike, and finally the end of the ridge at Nab Scar. From here, a steep descent leads to Rydal, where a track passes through Rydal Park, taking you back to Ambleside.

Looking ahead

Fairfield Horseshoe

The Fairfield Horseshoe is one of the best known ridge walks in the Lake District and as such is on every fell walker's 'must do' list. Its fame and popularity is well deserved, eight summits linked by a graceful undulating ridge with not too much height loss between and wide views in every direction. Satisfaction guaranteed.

In spring, watch for wheatears returning from overwintering in Africa to feed on the short turf of these high ridges.

Wheatear

Into the cloud: *A fell runner heading along the high, rock-strewn ridge*

The Walk

1. Leave the car park over the **footbridge** and cross the road. Turn left, then immediately right uphill on the 'Kirkstone Pass' road. Take the first left turning and keep to the left when the lane forks. Walk down **Nook Lane**, signposted for 'Low Sweden Bridge'.

Continue to **Nook End Farm**, go through gates to the right of the farmhouse, and cross the farmyard.

Continue along the track to cross **Low Sweden Bridge**.

2. Continue on the broad rising track, eventually passing through a gate in the wall. Curve to the left, with the wall on your the left, and continue through two wall gaps.

Bear left at a fork just after the second gap, and continue along the ridge with the wall on your left.

Continue to a **cairn at the base of crags**, and scramble up a tricky step beside the wall. (The step can be avoided by cutting right, up the rocks, just before it). Carry on beside the wall, go through a gap, and continue over broken ground. Leave the wall for a while to avoid boggy ground. Return to the wall, go through a low gap, and climb to a cairn.

Bear left, a little further on, leaving the good path and taking a fainter one that stays with the wall and climbs to **Low Pike summit**.

3. From the cairn, head east, dropping down to curve left below the summit. Descend to a saddle, and cross a stile over a wall. When the wall on the left ends against crags, step over it, and continue on the other side; the wall reappears on your right. Stay beside the wall, eventually passing through a gap, to reach the **summit cairn on High Pike**.

Return to the wall, staying on the right of it now, dropping briefly before climbing steeply. As the angle eases, the wall becomes broken; continue on the path to the rocky **summit of Dove Crag**.

4. Descend on the right of the broken wall to a saddle. Climb steep rough ground, with the wall still on the left, to the twin cairns on the **summit of Hart Crag**.

The Fairfield massif: *A walker watches as Fairfield and Great Rigg emerge from the cloud*

Descend on a good path to a high-level saddle. Continue in the same direction, climbing steeply over a **rocky knoll**, to curve left and walk across the **Fairfield** summit plateau. Curve right along the path to reach the **summit**, where there is a **stone wind shelter**.

5. From the summit, head south across the plateau (in the direction of distant Windermere) to pick up the ridge path. Follow this path along the broad ridge to the **summit of Great Rigg** — a straightforward 1 kilometre/¾ mile.

6. Continue south along the ridge from Great Rigg — easy walking all the way — to a broad saddle before the short climb to Heron Pike. Climb steadily from the saddle leaving the main path beyond a **little tarn** on the left, to take a fainter path, half-left, to **Heron Pike's north top**. Continue on the fainter path, to rejoin the main path. Drop down, then climb again, to reach **Heron Pike south summit**.

7. From Heron Pike the ridge path continues in the same direction — still

easy and straightforward — to pick up a broken wall on the right. Continue to **Nab Scar,** and then meander along the summit ridge to a **cairn** where the old wall ends.

8. Continue ahead, crossing a stile in the wall, to follow the path beyond, now with a wall on the right. Drop steeply down the zig-zag path, which lower down joins a walled track. Continue along the track towards buildings below. Descend to pass through a gate and walk down a drive to a lane.

9. Turn right along the lane to the entrance to **Rydal Hall**. Turn left, on a footpath signposted to 'Ambleside'. Follow the track to the left of the buildings, and then right and left, past a **teashop**.

Cut left through the **campsite**, following the signs, and continue through a gate beside a stile. Follow the track ahead through **Rydal Park** to the main **A591** beside the **old lodge**.

Cross the road, and turn left along the pavement back into **Ambleside**, to complete the route. ♦

On the first half of the Kentmere Horseshoe

Kentmere Horseshoe

Garburn Pass – Yoke – Ill Bell – Froswick – Thornthwaite Crag – High Street – Nan Bield Pass – Kentmere Pike

What to expect:
High-level walking on broad grassy and rocky ridges. Good paths

Distance: 21 kilometres/13 miles

Ascent/descent: 1,210 metres/3,910 feet

Start: Limited parking in Kentmere village. A handful of cars can be parked by the institute by the church. Begin the walk by the church

Grid ref: NY 457 041

Ordnance Survey Map: OL 7 The English Lakes South-eastern area. *Windermere, Kendal & Silverdale*

Wainwrights: Yoke, Ill Bell, Froswick, Thornthwaite Crag, High Street, Mardale Ill Bell, Harter Fell, Kentmere Pike, Shipman Knotts

Walk outline

Easy walking from Kentmere village on a bridleway leads onto the broad ridge. A steeper rise to the first summit is followed by superb ridge walking on good paths with extensive views. The second half of the horseshoe is less interesting and can be left out if needed, but this would change the character of the walk. The final few miles are easy with the gradual descent of a broad gentle ridge with farm tracks back to Kentmere.

Kentmere Horseshoe

This route is a ridge walker's dream. Once the main ridge is gained most of the work is done and you can enjoy miles of elevated walking on good paths with minimal effort between summits and stunning views west towards Helvellyn and St Sunday Crag, and southwest to the long finger of Windermere. Although quite a long circuit, there is minimal rise and fall between each summit and with good paths under foot the miles slip by surprisingly easily. The second half of the horseshoe can be left out with an easier return along the valley from the Nan Bield Pass if needed.

In summer, the skyward trill of skylarks sometimes fills the air on Lakeland's high fells, lifting the spirits.

Summit of High Street

Skylark

Distant summits: *Looking back to Froswick and Ill Bell from the approach to High Street*

The Walk

1. From the **church** follow the lane away from the village and take the first lane on the left. In about 150 metres, and immediately after the house '**Green Head**' on the right, turn right onto the path signed for '**Garburn Pass**'. The path rises as a wide **cobbled track** (an old lane over the fells to Troutbeck), passing a huge boulder in the field on the left known as '**Badger Rock**', a well known local landmark.

Follow the track up onto the rounded crest of the ridge where you pass through a gate almost at the highest point. In 100 metres or so, turn right on a grass path that heads directly across the boggy, sloping moors roughly parallel to the **wall** away to the right. Further on, the path runs close by the wall and you meet a broad surfaced path that continues the climb to the first summit of the day — **Yoke**.

This summit is a broad grassy plateau marked by a single cairn, but it gives you your first proper views of the ridge ahead, and the fine shapely summit of Ill Bell.

2. The well-made path continues along the narrowing ridge crest to the **summit of Ill Bell** with its collection of stone cairns and view down to the **Kentmere Reservoir**.

Almost the entire walk can now be seen — the continuation to Froswick and Thornthwaite Crag, and High Street at the head of the Kentmere valley, and the second half of the ridge beyond the Nan Bield Pass over Harter Fell and Kentmere Pike.

The path continues over the less interesting summit of **Froswick** then along the connecting ridge to **Thornthwaite Crag** where the line of the old **Roman road** reaches the ridge from Troutbeck.

Thornthwaite Crag is an expansive summit with a tall stone cairn. Like Ill Bell it would be hard to mistake this top even in the poorest visibility. In clear weather its central location gives it grand views west to Helvellyn, St Sunday Crag and Dove Crag, and north down to Ullswater. South, the view includes Ill Bell and Froswick rising above the Kentmere valley.

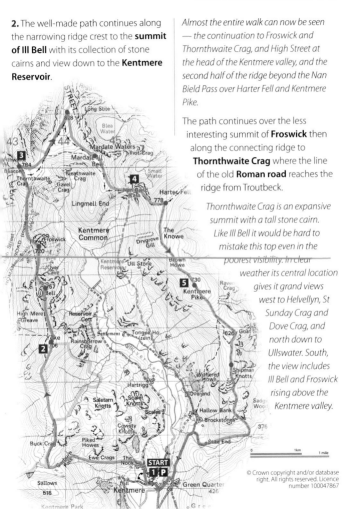

Ridge walker's dream: *Once the climbing is done you can enjoy miles of elevated walking*

3. From Thornthwaite Crag the path curves east, then north with views down to **Hayeswater**. The main path is approximately on the line of the Roman road here and is probably wide enough to accommodate a marching army. As you approach **High Street**, break away right to reach the summit marked by an **Ordnance Survey triangulation pillar**.

Views from the summit are restricted by the wide flat expanse of grass, but a short walk east to the lip of Blea Water Crag gives a grand view down into the head of Mardale

with both Blea Water and Haweswater visible below.

Bear right now along the edge of the broken cliffs that fall to **Blea Water** to the next summit — **Mardale III Bell** — an indistinct rise on the broad moors but with excellent views left to the northern slopes of High Street rising above Blea Water — the deepest tarn in the Lake District at 63 metres/207 feet. A little further on the path drops to **Nan Bield Pass**, an ancient route over the fells marked by a s**quare stone wind shelter**.

(The walk could be cut short here if

necessary by following the zig-zag path to the right. This heads across the slopes of Harter Fell above the Kentmere Reservoir, then along the valley bottom to join the lane end near the farms of Hallow Bank and Brockstones. Follow the lane back to Kentmere.)

4. The climb out of the Nan Bield Pass to the broad summit of **Harter Fell** is soon over. The highest point is marked by a **cairn** and close by is a **fence** which divides the broad ridge.

Follow the path right beside the fence for almost 2 kilometres/1¼ miles, the slight fall and rise to **Kentmere Pike** barely noticed.

5. From Kentmere Pike the path continues beside the wall southeast for just over 1 kilometre/¾ mile to cross a ladder stile in a crossing wall. **Shipman Knotts**, little more than a slight rise on the ridge, marks the final summit of the day. From here the path continues south beside the wall to join the **old track** linking Kentmere with Longsleddale. Turn right and follow the track down to the tarmac lane in the **Kentmere** valley. Turn left along the lane for about 1 kilometre/¾ mile and take the first lane on the right. Follow this down to the T-junction and turn right to return to the church to complete the route. ♦

Sunrise over Fairfield seen from St Sunday Crag

Deepdale Horseshoe

Patterdale – Birks – St Sunday Crag – Deepdale Hause –
Cofa Pike – Fairfield – Hart Crag – Hartsop Above How

What to expect:
Steep ascent on good
paths. High-level stony
and grassy paths

Distance: 14.5 kilometres/9 miles

Ascent/descent: 1050 metres/3,400 feet

Start: Small pay and display car park opposite the 'Patterdale Hotel', Patterdale

Grid ref: NY 396 159

Ordnance Survey Map: OL 5 The English Lakes North-eastern area. *Penrith, Patterdale & Caldbeck*

Wainwrights: St Sunday Crag, Fairfield, Hart Crag, Hartsop Above How (Birks optional)

Walk outline

After a gentle start in Patterdale, a steep climb up Thornhow
End takes you onto the broad stocky summit ridge of St
Sunday Crag with its superb views of Helvellyn and its
impressive eastern ridges. With much of the height gained the
walking is easier along the ridge with a short simple scramble
over Cofa Pike to reach Fairfield's broad summit plateau. The
broad ridge is followed to Hart Crag, then abandoned in
favour of the long gentle arm of Hartsop Above How with its
excellent views into the wilds of upper Deepdale.

Cofa Pike

Deepdale Horseshoe

Fairfield sits at the centre of a complex of fells, ridges and
dales running to all points of the compass. With several
close neighbours — some major summit themselves —
the Fairfield group is perfect for ridge walking and boasts
two of the best 'horseshoe' rounds in the region: the
Fairfield Horseshoe, which takes in the southern ridges
centred on Rydal, and the Deepdale Horseshoe to the
northeast.

This is the realm of ravens whose deep, guttural calls often
echo from the cliffs and rocks.

Raven

Steep ascent: *Tackling the initial climb onto the shoulder of Birks*

The Walk

1. From the car park cross the road and walk through the **hotel car park** keeping to the right of the main building. Take the signed footpath behind the hotel which passes through a small **wood** to a kissing gate. Go through the gate and bear right to follow a contouring path for about 1 kilometre/¾ mile.

At a path junction immediately below the steep, blunt ridge of **Thornhow End** (grid ref: NY 387 157), turn left. The path is steep and gains height quickly with widening views as you climb, both behind to the curve of Ullswater and right into the deepening shadowy depths of Grisedale and across to the bulk of Birkhouse Moor and Striding Edge.

2. Higher up the angle eases and the path heads for the shoulder of **Birks**, reaching the ridge midway between Birks and St Sunday Crag. (Birks can be reached easily by an out-and-back walk along the ridge to the left.)

Continue to climb directly up the broad ridge to the summit of **St Sunday Crag**.

St Sunday Crag is superb for views down into Grisedale and across to the edges of Helvellyn, Nethermost Pike and Dollywaggon Pike, as well as across Deepdale to the northern cliffs of Fairfield and Hart Crag.

3. The path crosses the broad summit dome in a southwest direction making the short descent to **Deepdale Hause**, where the paths from Grisedale and Deepdale meet.

The continuation to Fairfield is up a broken rocky ridge; a steadying hand needed here and there as you scramble up and over the rocky summit of **Cofa Pike**. It is a short climb now to the broad, bulky **summit of Fairfield**.

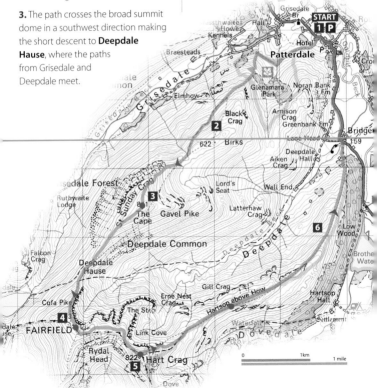

Mountain views: *Part of the expansive view from St Sunday Crag looking ahead to Fairfield with Seat Sandal, Dollywaggon Pike, Nethermost Pike and Helvellyn to the right separated from Fairfield by Grisedale Hause and Grisedale Tarn*

4. Fairfield sits at the junction of several ridges and provides the highpoint of both this round and the more famous Fairfield Horseshoe. *Its broad summit plateau dominates the valley heads of both Rydal Beck and Deepdale and gives grand views of virtually every fell in the Lake District.* The summit itself is close to the northern crags and is marked by a modest **stone wind shelter**.

To continue, head southeast for a few hundred metres, then pick up the broad path that swings east, then southeast along the broad ridge, soon with views right into Rydal. There is a short descent into the gap of **Link Hause** before the rise to **Hart Crag**, the third major summit of the day.

Like Fairfield, Hart Crag is a broad, stony summit and it is not always easy to decide on the highest point (just to the right of the main path).

5. The main ridge path continues southeast to **Dove Crag**, but our way heads northeast aiming for the long

finger-like edge of **Hartsop Above How**. In clear conditions you will be able to see the lower section of the ridge below and you should have no problem locating it, but things will be more tricky in poor visibility.

Head northeast (on a bearing of approx. 60 degrees) from the summit to locate the cairned path that descends through steep rocky ground. Once over this, the long central section of the ridge is straightforward and enjoyable.

6. Lower down a **wall** follows the ridge crest. Stay within sight of this on the right until you are almost at the bottom of the ridge approaching woods ahead. The path trends left away from the wall here to reach a small **gate** in the fence. Go through the gate and walk down through **woods** to go through a second gate into a large field. Go ahead across the field to a farm track and follow this rightwards to the road at **Deepdale Bridge**.

Turn left along the road and return past the **Youth Hostel** to **Patterdale** to complete the route. ♦

High Stile from Buttermere

The **High Stile** ridge

Buttermere – Scarth Gap – Seat – High Crag – High Stile – Red Pike – The Saddle – Dodd – Birtness Woods

What to expect:
Rough, steep walking to gain a high, broad ridge. Steep descent

Distance: 12.25 kilometres/7¾ miles

Ascent/descent: 1,050 metres/3,430 feet

Start: The village of Buttermere where there are two official car parks

Grid ref: NY 175 169

Ordnance Survey Map: OL 4 The English Lakes North-western area. *Keswick, Cockermouth & Wigton*

Wainwrights: High Crag, High Stile, Red Pike

Walk outline

Pleasant lakeside walking from Buttermere village to the head of the lake is followed by a moderate ascent to Scarth Gap. A steep climb on good paths then takes you onto the High Crag– High Stile ridge. Walking along the ridge is straightforward and easy-angled and there are grand views to Buttermere, Crummock Water and into Ennerdale. Descent from the ridge is by a steep, pitched path that needs care in wet conditions.

The High Stile ridge

There are few lakes so dominated by the fells than Buttermere is by the High Stile group. In just over 1 kilometre/¾ mile, High Stile's steep northeastern slopes tumble over 600 metres to the wooded shores of the lake giving it the feel of a Norwegian fjord.

The central location allows magnificent views over many of the other Lakeland fells, particularly the nearby giants of the Scafell group. The walk along the ridge is characterised, too, by the ever-present bird's eye view down to Buttermere and Crummock Water. In summer, the lower slopes of these fells are bright with heather in bloom.

Buttermere pines

Heather

The Walk

1. From the centre of **Buttermere village**, take the road beside the 'Bridge Hotel' and keep to the left of the 'Fish Hotel' towards the lake. Just before the lake, turn right to cross the footbridge over **Buttermere Dubs** — the outflow from Buttermere — and a second footbridge over **Sourmilk Gill**. Go through the hand gate and take the good path through the **conifer woods** close to the lake shore.

There are good views from occasional breaks in the trees across to the house of Hassness in its wooded gardens and up to Fleetwith Pike dominating the valley head.

Beyond the woods and just before you reach the head of the lake, the path splits. Most traffic will keep ahead on the popular lakeside trail, but our way heads right on the path that climbs diagonally up towards **Scarth Gap** (about 1.5 kilometres/1 mile).

At Scarth Gap the hoped for view into the wilds of Ennerdale

Final summit: *The setting sun catches the slopes of Dodd with Grasmoor behind*

is not realised, the little pass being hemmed in on both sides. Great Gable and the rather unimpressive Kirk Fell are the only summits of note visible.

2. The main pitched path bears left onto Haystacks now, but our way heads right up onto the little **summit of Seat**, which gives you your first view of Ennerdale and Pillar. *This is a better place for a stop than Scarth Gap, the views are wider and the crowds heading for Haystacks are now behind you.*

The path dips a little after Seat, then climbs over 200 metres up **Gamlin End** to the summit of **High Crag**. This looks steep and it is!

The good news is that once the ascent to High Crag is behind you, so is most of the hard work. The ridge ahead to **High Stile** is mainly level with just 50 metres ascent in a little over 1 kilometre/¾ mile, so stride out and enjoy the superb scenery on both sides of the ridge.

To the right there are grand views into the shadowy depths of Burtness Combe and down to Buttermere lake more than 600

Birds' eye view: *The view down to Buttermere is a constant companion from the ridge*

---

metres below. The view left is out along the glacial trough of Ennerdale with the bulk of Pillar rising across the valley. Its famous rock, from which the whole mountain takes its name, is in the centre of the face directly below the summit.

As you reach the summit of High Stile, walk ahead to the rim of the combe for one of the best views in the area. This takes in the full length of Crummock Water seen against the striking profiles of Red Pike and its smaller neighbour Dodd. It is also worth the short detour north for the view down

the ridge to Buttermere village over 700 metres below.

3. The continuation to **Red Pike** is just as straightforward and follows the rim of the combe with fine views all the way. There is more grass on this section with just a short rise to the little **stone wind shelter** marking the highest point.

4. The initial descent northeast down the ridge from Red Pike is steep and very loose and requires care, but it is a short descent and soon you are on the easier ground of **The Saddle** — the broad rounded pass between Red Pike and the small **summit of Dodd**. (This top is a short out-and-back detour and

well worth it for the fine view down to Crummock Water and up to Fleetwith Pike at the head of the valley.)

The path cuts diagonally down from The Saddle to cross **Sourmilk Gill**, the outflow stream from the tarn, then begins the steep descent to Birtness Woods by a tiring, pitched path that requires care when wet.

After crossing the stream, the path swings leftwards coming close to the stone wall over on the left beside the stream. The pitching begins here and initially the angle is not great, but lower down it steepens considerably.

The reddish rock that gives the fell its name, is notoriously slippery when wet and on the steep sections the rocks have been placed parallel with the slope rather than forming steps.

This path will not end soon enough, but by the time you enter **Birtness Woods** by the small gate the worst is behind you. The path cuts directly down through the trees and eventually joins the lakeside path beside the footbridge crossed earlier.

Retrace the outward path back to Buttermere village to complete the route. ♦

Grisedale Pike

Coledale Horseshoe

Braithwaite – Grisedale Pike – Hopegill Head – Coledale Hause – Eel Crag – Sail – Scar Crags – Causey Pike

What to expect:
A mixture of grassy and rocky fell paths. Long ridge walk, several ascents/descents

Distance: 17 kilometres/10½ miles

Ascent/descent: 1,115 metres /3,660 feet

Start: There is limited free parking in an old quarry on the lefthand side of the Whinlatter Pass road (the B5292) north of Braithwaite

Grid ref: NY 227 237

Ordnance Survey Map: OL 4 The English Lakes North-western area. *Keswick, Cockermouth & Wigton*

Wainwrights: Grisedale Pike, Hopegill Head, Eel Crag, Sail, Scar Crags, Causey Pike

Walk outline

Good paths abound on the Coledale Horseshoe and the three mile ascent from Braithwaite to Grisedale Pike is no exception. With most of the hard work behind you, a good path then takes you along Hobcarton Crag to Hopegill Head with a drop to Coledale Hause. A climb of roughly five hundred feet on good paths and you are on the high point of the day: Eel Crag, at the head of Coledale. From here, a grassy ridge takes you down the southern side of the valley, crossing Sail, Scar Crags and Causey Pike, before an exciting descent and a bit of road walking brings you back to Braithwaite.

Hopegill Head

Coledale Horseshoe

The traditional circuit leaves the high level route at Sail Pass, descending to cross High Moss and returning by the Outerside to Barrow ridge. While this gives a genuine round of Coledale, it misses out three great summits that make a complete high-level horseshoe. In contrast, this extended Coledale round follows the skyline higher up to include Sail, Scar Crags and Causey Pike. On a warm day you'll be able to watch buzzards searching for thermals.

Buzzard

The Walk

1. Leave the car park up steps signposted to 'Grisedale Pike'. Curve left near a **conifer plantation**, and climb up to cross a stile in the fence. Continue ahead and stay right when the path forks. Keeping the trees on your right, climb steeply up the broad path.

When the trees end, walk ahead. The path levels along the **Kinn Ridge**, before descending into a shallow saddle. Follow the path up onto **Sleet How**

to curve left along the narrowing east ridge, with a final steep and airy rise to **Grisedale Pike summit**.

2. From Grisedale Pike, descend to the southwest beside a broken wall. Drop left on a steep section, trending back to the right, to pick up the wall again. Cross a saddle, climbing up and over **Hobcarton Crag**.

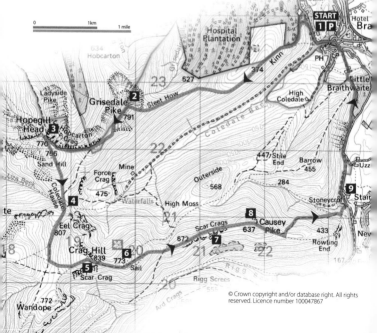

© Crown copyright and/or database right. All rights reserved. Licence number 100047867

The final summit: *Looking along the ridge from Scar Crags to Causey Pike*

Descend steeply to the saddle below **Hopegill Head,** bearing right at a **cairn** where the path forks. Climb the path above the north face of Hopegill Head, continuing to the **cairn on the rocky summit**.

3. Backtrack a little before branching off to the right, southwards, crossing **Sand Hill** on a broad path. Descend to **Coledale Hause,** at first on scree and then on grass.

4. As you cross the broad saddle, keep to the left when the path forks, curving to the right beneath the rocks of Eel Crag. Ignore the path to the left, instead picking up a path beside the gill, heading south up the narrowing valley between Eel Crag and Grasmoor. At a **grassy saddle**, go left at a junction of paths, climbing to the **summit of Eel Crag (Crag HIll on the map)** on a path that's well cairned higher up.

5. Leave the summit **triangulation pillar**, heading southeast now, following a faint path that soon develops and

High-level ridge: *Leaving Grisedale Pike, heading for Hopegill Head and Eel Crag*

curves down a rocky ridge above Scott Crag. Cross a small saddle, continuing ahead uphill towards the top of **Sail**. Cut left here, leaving the main path. The angle soon eases to reach the **summit cairn**.

6. Return to the main path a little further on, and turn left along it. Descend to cross over a saddle, and continue ahead at the junction of paths, before climbing up to the ridge of **Scar Crags**. Follow a fainter path to the **summit cairn**.

7. Continue eastwards, descending over the final saddle of the day, then climb steeply uphill over several bumps to **Causey Pike**.

8. Care is needed descending from Causey Pike in the direction of **Rowling End** below.

The initial descent down a steep rock rib is scrambly and exposed. Ignore the gully on the left, staying on the main rocks and dropping down to pick up a good path. Follow this down to a **cairn**, going left where the path forks, before descending to the left of Rowling End in the direction of **Stoneycroft Gill**.

Walk down this path towards **Stoneycroft Farm**, keeping the gill below to your left. When the path forks, bear left, descending to the road beside a **bridge**.

9. Turn left over the bridge and follow the road past a parking area on the right and a quarry on the left.

Shortly before a plantation, turn left at a bridleway sign. Rise through gorse to the left of the plantation with a wall on your right. Climb over the end of the long northeast ridge of **Barrow** before descending across open ground to a

gate. Walk down the next field to cross a stile between **farm buildings**. Curve right and left in front of the farm, then walk down the access track to the road.

(Alternatively you can cut this last section out and continue along the lane to Braithwaite.)

Turn left into **Braithwaite** and cross the bridge. Follow the road signposted to 'Whinlatter Pass', rising to turn left at a T-junction. Walk uphill along the busy road back to the quarry car park to complete the walk. ♦

High Snab Bank and Robinson from the Newlands road

Little Dale Round

Newlands Church – High Snab Bank – Robinson – Little Dale Edge – Hindscarth – Scope End – Low Snab

What to expect:
Narrow grassy ridges and broad summit plateau. A mix of grassy and stony paths

Distance: 10.5 kilometres/6½ miles

Ascent/descent: 790 metres/2,590 feet

Start: Free parking in a parking area on the minor road near Chapel Bridge, south of the hamlet of Little Town. This soon fills up, so get there early

Grid ref: NY 232 194

Ordnance Survey Map: OL 4 The English Lakes North-western area. *Keswick, Cockermouth & Wigton*

Wainwrights: Robinson, Hindscarth

Walk outline

After passing the beautiful Newlands Church, quiet lanes, access tracks and mountain paths take the walker onto the narrow ridge of High Snab Bank, where you can also enjoy a scramble up several rocky steps before the summit of Robinson is reached. The route stays high around Little Dale Edge to the summit of Hindscarth with a return along the wonderful Scope End ridge to complete an atmospheric and classic Lakeland horseshoe walk.

Little Dale Round

Robinson and Hindscarth enclose the hidden valley of Little Dale and are very similar in character, especially their northeast ridges. Both High Snab Bank and Scope End are classic Lakeland ridges — long and narrow with stunning views down either side. Views into the Buttermere valley can be enjoyed from Robinson, and to the Honister Pass and Newlands from Hindscarth.

You're likely to be accompanied all day by that ubiquitous 'little brown bird' of the uplands, the meadow pipit.

Newlands Church

Meadow pipit

Starting out: *Easy walking on High Snab Bank, approaching Robinson*

The Walk

1. Leave the parking area and turn left over **Chapel Bridge**. Take the turning on the left signed to 'Newlands Church ¼ mile – No Through Road' and walk down the road to **Newlands Church**.

2. Ignore a left turn, and continue past the church with **Keskadale Beck** to your right. The farm road climbs gradually to a National Trust sign on the right for **'High Snab Farm'**. Keep ahead here. Higher up, go through a gate passing **Low High Snab** on the left. The track becomes rougher, passing through a gate after the buildings. Continue

through another gate and carry on into **Little Dale**.

When the wall on the right ends, turn right, off the track, on a path that rises half-left steeply uphill, passing to the left of conifers. Continue climbing, to gain the ridge of **High Snab Bank**.

Walk left along the grassy crest of the ridge with grand views.

At the end of the ridge, the higher slopes of Robinson rise more steeply and four rocky steps have to be scrambled over. The path remains good and the way over the rocks is easy to follow. Stay on the main path above the scramble, ignoring any right turnings, to the **summit of Robinson**.

Continue over the summit area to the twin rock outcrops that mark the highest point.

3. Head south from Robinson, reaching a cairn near the **ridge fence**. Bear left on the path beside the fence. Descend to the grassy saddle of **Littledale Edge** at the head of Little Dale, where the path forks.

Take the lefthand fork, rising towards Hindscarth. The path curves to the right and peters out. Walk a few paces forward to another path and bear left to reach the **Hindscarth summit cairn**.

4. Leave the summit, heading north for a large **cairn-cum-shelter**. Pass this, dropping steeply down the hillside to join the narrow ridge of **Scope End**.

A delightful ridge path follows, sticking mostly to the crest. The final section of the ridge undulates before dropping steeply to arrive at a T-junction of paths near a fence and wall.

5. Bear right, following the path to the right of a **farmhouse**. Beyond a **spoil heap**, curve left and descend to a track. Ignore the first footpath to the left, and take the permissive path signposted for 'Newlands Church', which heads left through the farmyard of **Low Snab**.

6. Follow the track beyond the farm to cross a **bridge**. When a lane joins from the left, continue ahead to reach **Newlands Church**. Turn right, back to the car park, to complete the walk. ♦

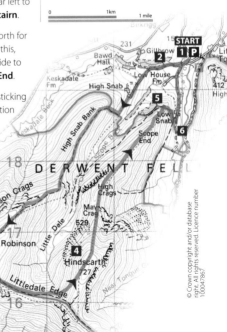

Looking down to The Rigg and Haweswater

High Street by Rough Crag

The Rigg – Rough Crag – Long Stile End – High Street – Rampsgill Head – Kidsty Pike – Kidsty Howes

What to expect:
A mixture of grassy and rocky fell paths on a broad ridge.

Distance: 10 kilometres/6½ miles

Ascent/descent: 850 metres/2,800 feet

Start: Car park at the head of Haweswater.

Grid ref: NY 469 107

Ordnance Survey Map: OL 5 The English Lakes North-eastern area. *Penrith, Patterdale & Caldbeck*

Wainwrights: High Street, Rampsgill Head, and Kidsty Pike

Walk outline

A long, but not too demanding walk up a distinctive ridge with fine views and a steep final climb to High Street. This is followed by straightforward walking around the deeply-cut Riggindale and over Kidsty Pike.

High Street

Think of High Street and no vivid mountain image comes to mind as it does with the mention of Blencathra, Skiddaw or the Langdale Pikes. High Street is hidden amongst the high moors of the northeastern fells: a high, Pennine-like plateau, cut by long glacial valleys but with no memorable skylines. Yet, up close, High Street provides fine drama, with narrow ridges, high crags and deep mountain lakes.

Without doubt, the finest approach to High Street is along the narrow edge of Rough Crag, the dramatic fall into Riggindale on one side and the spectacular amphitheatre holding Blea Water on the other.

The fells are home to that archetypal Lakeland breed of sheep, the tough, brown-woolled Herdwick.

The Rigg

Herdwick sheep

The Walk

1. Go through the **gate** at the end of the little car park and follow the broad path ahead. In 100 metres or so, at a path junction, turn right at the corner of the wall and follow the path over **two footbridges**. Bear right after the second bridge and soon you will be walking above the lake towards the wooded headland known as '**The Rigg**'. As you approach the woods the path bears left up to the crest of the ridge. Go through a gap in the wall and bear left almost immediately to start the long ascent of the **Rough Crag ridge**.

There are grand views down the length of Haweswater as well as down into Riggindale and across to the shapely summit of Kidsty Pike.

The path is easy and ascends with the wall on the left until it passes through a gap in the wall. Steeper now, the path climbs up to gain the crest again by the wall. Once you are over this section the walking is much easier and you can cruise along and enjoy the widening views on both sides.

To the left you will see the two tarns of Small Water and Blea Water in their dark glacial valleys. Blea Water's claim to fame is its depth — at 63 metres/207 feet, it is the deepest tarn in the Lake District by a long way and of the larger valley lakes is only exceeded in depth by Wast Water and Windermere.

2. A small cairn marks the **summit of Rough Crag** after which the ridge

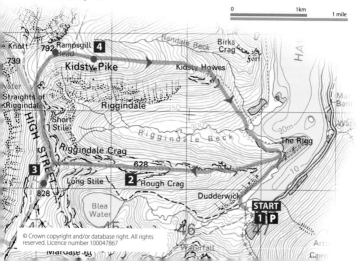

Ridge crest: *On the crest of Rough Crag looking to High Street*

drops to a small grassy saddle known as **Caspel Gate** where there is a **small pool**. Ahead the ridge steepens again for the final 200 metres climb up **Long Stile Edge** to the summit. The ridge is steep and rough but there is no difficulty and you are soon on the summit, its broad, grassy plateau coming as an anticlimax after the shapely ridge of the ascent.

3. The summit of **High Street** is marked by an Ordnance Survey **triangulation pillar**, but the views are better from here where you can look back down the ridge to Haweswater and into the shadowy depths of Blea Water over 300 metres below.

Head north on the good path along the ridge beside the wall and across the head of **Riggindale**, then bear northeast where the path forks to the broad bulky **summit of Rampsgill Head**. Continue to the fine little summit of **Kidsty Pike** with its superb views into Riggindale and across to Rough Crag and High Street.

4. From Kidsty Pike a good path descends almost due east for 1.5 kilometres/1 mile before heading down through the broken rocks of **Kidsty Howes**. Lower down, just above the lake, you pass close to **Randale Beck** on the left before bearing right to cross the **stone bridge** over **Riggindale Beck**. Follow the well-used footpath back beside the woods of **The Rigg** to complete the route. ♦

Looking down Mosedale to Yewbarrow from the shoulder of Pillar

Mosedale Horseshoe

Wasdale Head – Black Sail Pass – Pillar – Scoat Fell – Steeple – Red Pike – Yewbarrow

What to expect:
A long, spectacular ridge walk. High, rocky mountain paths. Short scramble

Distance: 17.25 kilometres/11 miles

Ascent/descent: 1,630 metres/5,350 feet

Start: There is a large parking area at Wasdale Green, about 400m before the famous 'Wasdale Head Inn'

Grid ref: NY 186 084

Ordnance Survey Map: OL 4 The English Lakes North-western area. *Keswick, Cockermouth & Wigton* and OL 6 The English Lakes South-western area. *Coniston, Ulverston & Barrow-in-Furness*

Wainwrights: Pillar, Scoat Fell, Steeple, Red Pike, Yewbarrow

Walk outline

A gradual climb on a good path from Wasdale Head to Black Sail Pass is followed by a high-level ridge walk over Pillar, Scoat Fell and the striking rock peak of Steeple. The broad ridge continues to Red Pike and finally a scramble both onto and off the superb little mountain of Yewbarrow to complete the round.

Mosedale Horseshoe

Wasdale Head is one of the most famous centres for walking and climbing in the region. Its reputation is well earned: it's the wildest valley head in the Lake District, surrounded by the highest summits. But most eyes turn to either Scafell Pike (the highest peak in England) or Great Gable, leaving one of the finest horseshoe walks in the region unnoticed and almost untouched little more than a stone's throw away.

Black Sail YHA

This is a superb route over high ground, gathering a fine collection of Lakeland summits along the way and enjoying unrivalled views of the Scafell group throughout.

Look out, too, for the elusive ring ouzel, a black bird with a white collar that nests among the rocks and boulder fields.

Ring ouzel

The Walk

1. From **Wasdale Green** follow the lane to the 'Wasdale Head Inn'. Turn left through the car park, past the **shop and bar**, and bear right beside the beck. Pass the picturesque little **stone bridge** continuing ahead between the beck and a farm on the right. Soon the path splits — bear left rising to a gate where the Mosedale path swings left again.

Soon you are in the wilds of Mosedale and you can appreciate just how large and impressive it is for the first time. At the head of the dale the south face of Pillar rises in a series of steep broken crags over 700 metres, with the craggy eastern face of Red Pike to the left.

The path soon curves rightwards to begin the long climb to **Black Sail Pass**. Once you have crossed **Gatherstone Beck** the view back down the valley becomes increasingly impressive as the northern

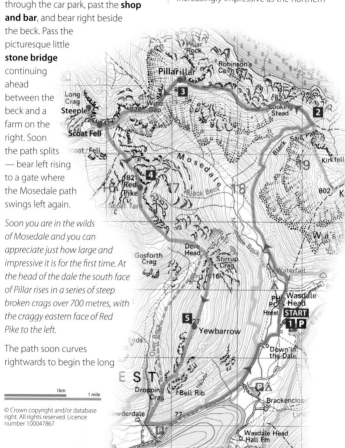

1km

1 mile

Rock peak: *Walkers detour from the main ridge to the spectacular rock peak of Steeple*

prow of Yewbarrow soars 500 metres above the beck.

2. As you reach the summit of the pass, the extensive view into Ennerdale is not realised, so head left along the ridge making the minor detour right to the **summit of Looking Stead** and all will be revealed — *the shadowy forested depths of Ennerdale, the Haystacks/ High Stile ridge, with Fleetwith Pike and the Robinson/Hinscarth ridge beyond. Southwards, is the striking prow of Yewbarrow.*

Continue steeply up the ridge from Looking Stead to the **summit of Pillar**, where you will enjoy spectacular views into both Ennerdale and Mosedale from the ridge.

Pillar has one of the best panoramas in the Lake District, a prospect dominated mainly by the jumbled, rocky mass of the Scafell group to the southeast, with the distinctive profile of Great Gable seen over the rounded back of Kirk Fell. Westwards, the view takes in the long glacial trough of Ennerdale culminating in Ennerdale Water with the Irish Sea in the distance.

Final summit: *Looking to Yewbarrow, the final summit in this long round, from Pillar, as the rising sun catches the ridge crest*

3. From Pillar, head southwest over the extensive summit plateau and descend into **Wind Gap**, the pass separating Pillar from Black Crag. The climb to **Black Crag** is broken and rocky but soon over and the remaining ridge to **Scoat Fell** is narrow and grassy with just a short rise over rocks to the summit, an unremarkable stony plateau.

The out-and-back extension to the superb summit of **Steeple** is recommended. The sight of Steeple as you approach along the ridge backed by Ennerdale and High Stile is one of the highlights of the walk.

Return to Scoat Fell and head southeast to pick up the ridge path to **Red Pike**. *Again the view is dominated by the Scafell group across the divide of Wasdale.*

4. The descent from Red Pike to the pass of **Dore Head** is a mix of grass and scree, a good, visible path all the way.

(The Yewbarrow scramble can be by-passed here by turning right and following the path above Over Beck.)

The ascent of **Yewbarrow** is a straightforward walk up the broken, loose slope to begin the short scramble

onto the ridge. The easiest line is on the left edge of the crags almost overlooking the drop into Mosedale. There is less exposure to the right but the scrambling is less straightforward.

The summit ridge gives unrivalled views of the Scafell group, Great Gable and Wast Water.

5. The descent is initially straightforward and heads down the narrowing ridge with superb views to Wast Water over 500 metres below. Lower down look for the point where the path breaks right above **Dropping Crag**. This is important as there is no walking route down the ridge crest from here.

The descent is now steep and loose and you may doubt you are in the right place, but the path is obvious and there is a short section of **formalised pitching** lower down.

At the bottom of the scree a path heads left through the bracken to cross a **ladder stile** on the grassy ridge crest. Head right down the grass path beside the wall to a second stile. Turn left here and follow the path down beside **Over Beck** to the little car park.

The return to Wasdale Head is unavoidably along the road — just over 2 kilometres/1½ miles to complete the route. ♦

Perfect conditions on Striding Edge

Striding & Swirral Edges

Patterdale – Lanty's Tarn – Hole-in-the-Wall – Striding Edge – Helvellyn – Swirral Edge – Catstycam – Glenridding

What to expect:
Spectacular rocky ridge scramble in ascent and descent. Good, well used fell paths

Distance: 12 kilometres/7½ miles

Ascent/descent: 960 metres/3,150 feet

Start: The National Park car park in the centre of Glenridding.

Grid ref: NY 385 169

Ordnance Survey Map: OL 5 The English Lakes North-eastern area. *Penrith, Patterdale & Caldbeck*

Wainwright summits: Helvellyn, Catstycam

Walk outline

Easy walking to Lanty's Tarn to gain the Grisedale path followed by a long moderate ascent to the ridge crest. Straightforward low-grade scrambling on a narrow rock ridge with some exposure to reach Helvellyn's high summit plateau. A shorter scrambling descent via Swirral Edge, then easier walking to the shapely summit of Catstycam. The long easy-angled Glenridding path provides a return route.

Striding Edge & Swirral Edge

The most famous and popular mountains and hills in any area are usually the highest — Snowdon in North Wales, Ben Nevis in Scotland — but in the Lake District Helvellyn seems to have jumped the queue and knocked Scafell Pike off the number one spot. One reason for this is undoubtedly the inaccessibility of the latter. Helvellyn, on the other hand, rises directly from a main road which runs through the heart of the district. It is also one of the four highest summits in the Lake District and it has perhaps the most famous ridge walk in the country — Striding Edge. This narrow airy arête is justifiably famous and provides one of the best mountain experiences to be had on the Lakeland fells.

On Swirral Edge

Lichen

On the edge: *Walkers following the narrow crest of Striding Edge*

The Walk

1. Leave the car park by the lower entrance and turn right along the road to cross the **bridge**. Turn right immediately (opposite the '**Glenridding Hotel**') and walk along the lane between the river and the shops. At the end of the access lane, go through the large gate ahead and in a few metres cross the **footbridge** on the left. Follow the **pitched footpath** up through woods and onto the open hillside.

2. At a gate in the wall ahead, don't go through; instead turn sharp left and follow the path up to **Lanty's Tarn**, in its small hollow and surrounded by pines.

Follow the path past the tarn, then bear right off the main path on a narrower footpath that heads across grass to enter and pass through a **small wood** by gates. Beyond the wood the path descends to join the main path coming up from **Grisedale**.

Grisedale is a beautiful valley and there are superb views from here up to the head of the dale to the shapely summits of

Nethermost Pike, Dollywaggon Pike and St Sunday Crag.

Turn right and follow the broad path climbing steadily up towards the famous '**Hole-in-the-Wall**' — a gap in the wall that can be seen running up the hillside to the skyline ahead. The path is never steep, but it is much further than it looks to the skyline (over 2 kilometres/1½ miles).

As you gain height there are increasing views left into Grisedale and up to the head of the valley.

The ridge crest is a good place for a break. Here the impressive east face of Helvellyn, with the enclosing arms of Striding Edge

and Swirral Edge, can be seen for the first time rising above Red Tarn which occupies the bottom of the combe (out of sight until you are further along the ridge).

3. Cross the stile here ('Hole in the Wall') and continue on the path ahead. **Striding Edge** starts with the small **summit of Low Spying How**, a good place to take stock of the ridge ahead.

The first section is composed of clean blocky rock with very little grass, the second half is narrower with a sharper crest but more broken rocks. **NB** – Nowhere is the scrambling 'difficult' but it is fairly exposed, so you will need good balance and a head for heights.

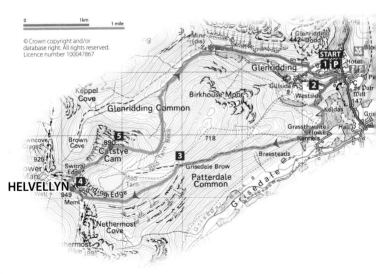

Mountain ridge: *Scramblers on the crest of Striding Edge with views across Grisedale to St Sunday Crag and Fairfield*

The less adventurous can avoid the crest by a traversing path a little way down on the right.

The final obstacle on the ridge provides the crux — a **squat rock tower** requiring a short scramble descent to a narrow gap at the point where the ridge merges into the broken upper slopes of the mountain. Easier scrambling, then steep scree lead onto the summit plateau where you will enjoy the fine classic view back along the ridge.

Head right along the plateau rim past the cross-shaped **stone wind shelter** to **Helvellyn summit** marked by a **triangulation pillar**.

Helvellyn is one of the few Lakeland summits where almost every other fell is visible. The most striking panorama is westwards, where you should be able to see the Coniston Fells, Bowfell, Crinkle Crags, Esk Pike and Scafell Pike. Great Gable is probably the most prominent and striking of all. The Derwent Fells and Skiddaw complete the view to the northwest.

4. Beyond the summit a small **cairn** marks the exit point from the plateau

onto **Swirral Edge**. This is both easier and shorter than Striding Edge, but still requires care. The broken rocks soon merge into grass as the angle eases on the broad saddle between Helvellyn and Catstycam.

A good path bears right from here to the outflow of **Red Tarn** where it joins the Glenridding path, but Catstycam is too good a summit to leave out and is easily gained by the gentle ridge ahead.

The view back to Helvellyn rising above Red Tarn from here is superb, particularly under winter conditions, or when late snow lingers on this sheltered northeast face.

5. From the **summit of Catstycam**, descend the rounded east ridge on the path that sweeps down to join the Glenridding path beside **Red Tarn Beck**.

Follow this path down beside the beck into the lower valley. The path then stays close to the broader **Glenridding Beck**. Cross the beck by the large **wooden footbridge** on the left and follow the path right, soon passing **Glenridding Youth Hostel** to join the unsurfaced lane which can be followed easily back to **Glenridding** to complete the route (about 2 kilometres/1½ miles). ♦

Scramblers on Sharp Edge

Blencathra's ridges

Scales – Mousthwaite Comb - Scales Tarn – Sharp Edge
Blencathra – Hall's Fell Ridge – Gate Gill – Doddick Gill

What to expect:
Spectacular rocky ridge scramble in ascent and descent with exposure. Good fell paths

Distance: 9 kilometres/5½ miles
Ascent/descent: 722 metres/2,370 feet
Start: Limited parking is available in a layby on the A66 at Scales (grid ref: NY 344 269). Alternatively there is a small parking area along the minor lane about 700 metres beyond the 'White Horse Inn' at Scales. Park immediately after the little bridge
Grid ref: NY 349 272
Ordnance Survey Map: OL 5 The English Lakes North-eastern area. *Penrith, Patterdale & Caldbeck*
Wainwrights: Blencathra (Hallsfell Top)

Walk outline

Initially steep walking on good footpaths leads over the broad grassy ridge of Scales Fell and beside the upper River Glenderamackin to reach the sheltered hollow containing Scales Tarn directly below Sharp Edge. Exposed scrambling on Sharp Edge takes you directly onto the summit plateau. Descent is by the easier but still rocky edge of Hall's Fell Ridge — a direct and spectacular 600 metre line down the mountain's southern face. Easy walking to finish.

Scales Tarn

Blencathra's ridges

Blencathra is the great mountain bulk that greets the motorist entering the Lake District from the northeast along the A66. And what a greeting — no gentle introductions, this mountain hits you like a fist and reveals all in a magnificent medley of ridges and buttresses.

This route uses easy access from the A66 for a classic round via Sharp Edge and Hall's Fell Ridge. Sharp Edge is one of the best low-end scrambles in the Lake District and takes a direct line up a narrow rock ridge. If you enjoy Sharp Edge, Hall's Fell Ridge provides the logical descent being easier and less exposed, but still providing interesting scrambling.

Peregrine and prey

The Walk

1. From the main road follow the lane past the '**White Horse Inn**' and just before it bends left down to cross a stream, take the signed path on the left.

The path is well used and obvious and heads up the lefthand side of the little valley of **Mousthwaite Comb**, before swinging diagonally-right across the steep valley head to the broad saddle on the skyline.

The saddle is a good place to take a breather and survey the route ahead.

Sharp Edge can be seen rising impressively above the upper valley of the River Glenderamackin with the rounded, grassy shoulder of Scales Fell to the left.

2. The path swings left now along the broad grassy saddle towards **Scales Fell** and in about 400 metres forks. The path ahead continues up the broad, gentle slopes of Scales Fell to reach the summit. **Note:** *If you have any doubts about Sharp Edge, this is a straightforward route to the summit.*

For **Sharp Edge** branch right at the fork and follow the path on a contouring line up the valley towards the saddle on the skyline separating

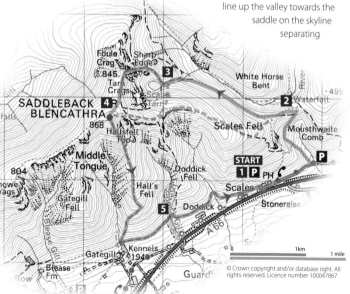

Almost there: *Looking down the final section of Sharp Edge ridge scramble*

Blencathra from **Bannerdale Crags**, with the beck down to the right.

About halfway up the valley the path crosses **Scales Beck**, which cascades out of the unseen hollow above. Cross the stream, then bear left up the pitched path beside the beck to **Scales Tarn**.

3. Over 150 metres above the tarn, **Sharp Edge** strikes an impressive skyline fringed by broken rock slabs and steep screes. Head right up the steep approach path to the start of the ridge.

(If you have a change of heart, the path up steps to the left will take you up the easier Scales Fell route.)

Scrambling is easy at first and begins up a 'V' shaped groove to reach the narrow crest. The ridge crest is quite narrow and there is exposure on both sides, but the scrambling is straightforward and much of it can be walked with just the occasional steadying hand if you feel confident enough.

The central section resembles a rock pavement but the polished rock can be slippery in the wet. The crux comes

Ridge challenge?: *Sharp Edge is one of Lakeland's most challenging ridge scrambles*

just before the ridge joins the main bulk of the mountain where some **small pinnacles** must be passed. The easiest line bypasses them on the right by means of a sloping ledge which some may find intimidating on account of the drop into a gully on the right. This can be slippery in the wet and requires care. The alternative is by delicate moves over a considerable drop on the lefthand side of the crest.

This leads to a gap in the ridge before the final slabby rocks that lead up onto the summit. Either climb these direct on good rock with small holds, or a slightly easier line can be taken up a shallow gully a few metres to the right.

The scrambling ends almost on the summit plateau where a good path heads left along the top of **Tarn Crags** to the **summit of Blencathra**.

The view from here is superb — especially down the 600 metre south face of the mountain to the A66 and the greenery of Saint John's in the Vale. Just about every Lakeland fell of note is visible, from the Coniston Fells past Bowfell, Scafell Pike, Great Gable, the Buttermere and Derwent Fells, to the neighbouring giant of Skiddaw.

4. The 600-metre-long **Hall's Fell Ridge** makes the perfect descent, being easier and more straightforward than Sharp Edge with little, if any, of the latter's exposure. It is also easy to locate, even in poor visibility, as it falls directly from the summit. The upper half of the ridge contains almost all of the scrambling which can be varied at will or even avoided altogether by paths mainly to the left of the crest.

(The Scales Fell path [due east] is a straightforward alternative descent.)

The lower section of the ridge is steep rather than rocky, the path trending right to reach the stream of **Gate Gill** with walled fields ahead and a small wood. Don't cross the stream here, but instead turn sharp left and follow the good footpath parallel to the wall on the right.

5. After you cross the next stream (**Doddick Gill**), you will need to make an unexpected rise around the **walled fields** ahead to continue.

The final obstacle is a short scramble down a rock step to cross **Scaley Beck**. About 400 metres further on, take the path right, between cottages, to reach the main road where a left turn will take you back to the **White Horse Inn** to complete the route. ♦

Useful Information

Cumbria Tourism

Cumbria Tourism's official website covers everything from accommodation and events to attractions and adventure. **www.golakes.co.uk**

Lake District National Park

The Lake District National Park website also has information on things to see and do, plus maps, webcams and news. **www.lakedistrict.gov.uk**

Tourist Information Centres

The main TICs provide free information on everything from accommodation and travel to what's on and walking advice.

Ambleside	01539 432 582	tic@thehubofambleside.com
Bowness	01539 442 895	bownesstic@lake-district.gov.uk
Coniston	01539 441 533	mail@conistontic.org
Keswick	01768 772 645	keswicktic@lake-district.gov.uk
Penrith	01768 867 466	pen.tic@eden.gov.uk
Ullswater	01768 482 414	ullswatertic@lake-district.gov.uk
Windermere	01539 446 499	windermeretic@southlakeland.gov.uk

Emergencies

The Lake District is covered by twelve volunteer mountain rescue teams. In a real emergency:

1. Make a note of your location (with OS grid reference, if possible); the name, age and sex of the casualty; their injuries; how many people are in the group; and your mobile phone number.

2. Call 999 or 112 and ask for the Cumbria police, and then for Mountain Rescue.

3. Give them your prepared details.

4. Do NOT change position until contacted by the mountain rescue team.

Weather

Five day forecast for the Lake District: 0844 846 2444
www.lakedistrict.gov.uk/weatherline